Yorkshire Terriers

Sarah Frank

Lerner Publications • Minneapolis

Lerner Publications Company
A division of Lerner Publishing Group, Inc.
241 First Avenue North
Minneapolis, MN 55401 USA

For reading levels and more information, look up this title at www.lernerbooks.com.

Library of Congress Cataloging-in-Publication Data

Names: Frank, Sarah, author.
Title: Yorkshire terriers / Sarah Frank.
Description: Minneapolis : Lerner Publications, [2019] | Series: Lightning bolt books. Who's a good dog? | Audience: Age 6-9. | Audience: Grade K to 3. | Includes bibliographical references and index.
Identifiers: LCCN 2018004400 | ISBN 9781541538573 (lb : alk. paper)
Subjects: LCSH: Yorkshire terrier—Juvenile literature.
Classification: LCC SF429.Y6 F73 2019 | DDC 636.76—dc23

LC record available at https://lccn.loc.gov/2018004400

Manufactured in the United States of America
1-45040-35867-6/12/2018

Table of Contents

A Very Special Dog

Imagine a brave, bold pooch. Maybe a big dog comes to mind. But tiny dogs can be fearless too! The Yorkshire terrier is proof of that.

Yorkshire terriers often are called Yorkies. They are small but feisty. They are also as cute as a button. They weigh only about 7 pounds (3 kg).

Yorkies are up for fun and games just like any big dog!

Yorkies are more than just lap dogs. They are active, curious canines. Yorkies also have lots of spunk. They might walk right up to a much larger dog!

Could you fall in love with a Yorkie?

Yorkies may look like windup toys, but they are real dogs. They like doing all the things other dogs do. They especially love being with their owners. And their owners think they are the best.

The Yorkie Story

Dogs come in all shapes and sizes. The American Kennel Club (AKC) groups dogs according to things such as size or behavior. One of the AKC's groups is the toy group. Yorkies belong to this group.

All of these dogs
are in the toy group.

Dogs in the toy group do not look alike. Yet they have one thing in common. They are all tiny pooches.

Toy dogs come from many different parts of the world. Yorkies come from England. They were common household pets in that country by the nineteenth century.

Yorkies have a touch of royalty about them!

Yorkies are still common household pets. They are also hard workers. Some Yorkies work as therapy dogs. They visit hospitals and nursing homes. Patients pet them and feel better!

Is a Yorkie for You?

Yorkies are great. But that doesn't mean everyone should have one. Decide with a parent whether a Yorkie is for you.

This basket is big enough to hold two tiny Yorkies.

Do you live in an apartment or condo? Then you might not want a big dog. Instead, a Yorkie might be perfect. These dogs don't need a lot of space.

Lonely Yorkies can cause trouble.

Yorkies don't like being alone. Do you have lots of after-school activities? Is your home often empty? Then a Yorkie may not be the right fit.

Yorkies make good watchdogs. They will bark when someone comes near. They will bark if they sense danger. Don't want a dog that barks a lot? Then pass on a Yorkie.

What's all the noise about?!

Yorkies at Home

Does a Yorkie sound right for you? Then you are in luck. It's time to prepare for your new furry friend. Every dog needs supplies, such as a leash, toys, and doggy bowls.

Vets make sure dogs are healthy.

Your Yorkie also needs good dog food. A vet can suggest what to feed your pet. Have the vet examine your Yorkie too.

Make time for your Yorkie. Yorkies love to play fetch. And they need lots of grooming. Talk to your Yorkie while you brush it. You'll both enjoy the time together.

Get your Yorkie used to brushing while it's still a puppy.

You and your Yorkie will be forever friends.

Your Yorkie will rely on you. Be the best dog owner you can be. Be ready to be rewarded with lots of Yorkie kisses!

Doggone Good Tips!

- Wondering what to name your Yorkie? Here are some ideas: Elf, Diva, Ninja, Gizmo, Tinkerbell, Miss Pretty Paws, or Sparky.

- Yorkies often wear topknots. This doggy hairdo is a little like a ponytail. Gently gather the hair on top of your Yorkie's head, and fasten it with a rubber band. You can add a bow for extra flair!

- Puppies are fun, but older Yorkies also make great pets. Some of them are even house-trained. That means less work for your family. See if your local humane society has an adult Yorkie that's up for adoption.

Why Yorkies Are the Best

- Their hair is amazing! It looks and feels like human hair. It has unusual coloring too. A Yorkie's head and legs are tan. Its body and tail are steel blue. Cool!

- They love to be with you. Bring them to a Little League game. Tote them to a picnic. These pint-size pooches can go almost anywhere.

- One brave Yorkie was a war hero. Her name was Smoky. In World War II (1939–1945), she saved soldiers' lives. She dragged a special wire that the soldiers needed to communicate through an 8-inch-wide (20 cm), 60-foot-long (18 m) water pipe.

Glossary

American Kennel Club (AKC): an organization that groups dogs by breed

canine: a dog

feisty: very lively or frisky

grooming: cleaning, brushing, and trimming a dog's coat

therapy dog: a dog brought to nursing homes and hospitals to comfort patients

toy group: a group of different types of dogs that are all small in size

vet: a doctor who treats animals

Further Reading

American Kennel Club
http://www.akc.org

American Society for the Prevention of Cruelty to Animals
https://www.aspca.org

Finne, Stephanie. *Yorkshire Terriers*. Minneapolis: Checkerboard Library, 2015.

Fishman, Jon M. *Hero Therapy Dogs*. Minneapolis: Lerner Publications, 2017.

Gray, Susan H. *Yorkshire Terriers*. New York: AV2 by Weigl, 2017.

Index

Photo Acknowledgments

Image credits: Pawel Gaul/iStock/Getty Images, p. 2; BIGANDT.COM/Shutterstock.com, p. 4; Liliboas/iStock/Getty Images, p. 5; Newspix/Getty Images, p. 6; Rebecca Emery/Photodisc/ Getty Images, p. 7; Pawel Gaul/iStock/Getty Images, p. 8; Jagodka/Shutterstock.com, p. 9; Ianych/Shutterstock.com, p. 10; Libby Welch/Alamy Stock Photo, p. 11; Felix Mizioznikov/ Shutterstock.com, p. 12; Sbolotova/Shutterstock.com, p. 13; ti-ja/iStock/Getty Images, p. 14; iagodina/iStock/Getty Images, p. 15; Bulltus_casso/Shutterstock.com, p. 16; Phase4Studios/Shutterstock.com, p. 17; Gerard Brown/Dorling Kindersley/Getty Images, p. 18; Pavel L Photo and Video/Shutterstock.com, p. 19; Sbolotova/Shutterstock.com, p. 23.

Front cover: Eric Isselee/Shutterstock.com.

Main body text set in Billy Infant regular 28/36. Typeface provided by SparkType.